THE WILTED ONES

a poetry collection
by
Lynne Reeder

THE WILTED ONES

THE WILTED ONES

DEDICATION

to all of the children--
those from me,
those beside me,
those forever a part of me--
you are the warmth and water
that keep me from wilting.

thank you.

THE WILTED ONES

THE WILTED ONES
TABLE OF CONTENTS

these poems are like my heart: hope and heartache, grief and gratitude, worry and wonder all mixed together. because life doesn't come with sections or parts where we can easily file our experiences separately from one another. instead, it's all the soil we're rooted in.

to the literary elite/my words are for me	9
fate of a different kind	11
heartlines	13
excavation	15
dandelion crown	17
measuring infinity	19
writing	21
depression is not just the absence of happiness	23
it's the wilted ones who linger	25
spliced	27
on the other side of addiction	29
mirror mirror	31
you're still my favorite season	33
i am more than you know	35
american systemic	37
boys will be boys*	39
what once was lost	41
unbridling me	43
this is how i bloom	45

if your depression needs a chapbook	47
the art of being an alcoholic	49
the horticulture of the classroom	51
your heart is your home	53
the lessons i can't teach you	55
when trees guide us	57
redefining my savior complex	59
the damage that was done/the damage that he's doing	61
the divine	63
weeding the soul	65
inspiration is shaped like you	67
without you i'm just broken	69
dirges (o grandmother)*	71
the moon is a reflection	73
don't make your words only about them	75
love is a person, not a gender	77
heart watch	79
as simple as	81
hibernation	83
stay	85
the space inside of me	87

THE WILTED ONES

who is the real heroin(e) of your story	89
extinct	91
seasons	93
lightning bug	95
come home to yourself	97
acceptance	99
experimental	101
be patient with yourself	103
aspirate	105
territory*	107
the last place i looked	109
draft five	111
the strings that bind	113
thrift shop heart	115
prescribed	117
religion moves like you	119
repentance	121
nonverbal	123
remedy	125
love is blind	127
the legacy of your suicide	129
always, feel	131

THE WILTED ONES

what is & what shall never be	133
habits	135
centrifugal motion	137
identity theft	139
stargazer	141
hematoma	143
elegy for a worry	145
how to analyze a poem (or, how to diagnose the damage)*	147
inhabitant	149
tithing	151
colored*	153
the ruins	155
husband	157
home is a person you never knew	159
finis	161

The backsides of shorter poem pages have been left blank intentionally, to give you space to write your own thoughts, inspirations, reactions, emotions. color this book with yourself, please. make it breathe.

share your creations with thepoemreeder@gmail.com or tag @thepoemreeder on your social media post.

THE WILTED ONES

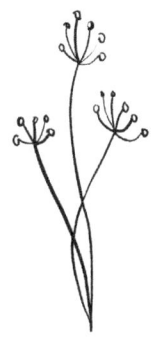

i am not your type of poet. i am too messy with my expression. my pages arrive to your hands damp and dripping. i have not always drained them through the sieve of stanzas or ever neatly baked them into bricks of blank verse. i tie them into tethered metaphors and soak them in my cheeks before spitting them into offerings for you. your taste buds don't know what to do with a girl like me who bleeds all over the recipe card. so you wipe up what i've spilled out and scrub it dry with your carefully crafted rejection letters. trying to reduce the heat under me. but don't you know paper only stokes a fire. so send me the generic template of your dismissal. because you aren't who i'm writing for anyway.

-to the literary elite/my words are for me

THE WILTED ONES

i think i loved you
because something in me knew
you'd be the kind of pain
i could turn into poetry

-fate of a different kind

THE WILTED ONES

the thing about paper conversations is that
they don't bleed the way speaking does.
the scraping of words from out of the throat
costs too much. the peeling of words
from fingertips, however,
is an act of giving.
come. hold my hand.
let me tell you who i am.

-heartlines

THE WILTED ONES

isn't it funny how
cracking the walls
around your heart
hardened the ones
around mine

-excavation

THE WILTED ONES

THE WILTED ONES

why do we wish upon
the very thing
we call weed
and rip out the roots
right beneath our own feet

-dandelion crowns

THE WILTED ONES

THE WILTED ONES

my oldest daughter loves math.
every birthday balloons into equations for her.
what year was Yaya born?
how old will I be in seventh grade?
mommy, how old are you?
my oldest daughter wants numbers
but I speak a different language.
i smooth her tangled hair and straighten the dreamcatcher she has pinned
    to the headboard of her bed.
i am autumn leaf old, child.
i am broken crayons and Sunday mornings and sweater blankets old.
i am dyed hair and black leggings and just one more chocolate old.
i am missing sweet tea at my grandmother's kitchen table,
i am my grandmother's kitchen table in our dining room because she is no
    longer here to give it a home years old.
i am thousands of students years old.
i am ancient as the pale blue of your irises.
i am still a child myself.
i am one moment at a time years old.
i am questions that have no answers old.
i am old enough to know what it is you're really asking
but instead I smile as I pick up your worn teddy bear, the one threadbare at
    the seams and missing his eyes, the Tiresias prophet of our house, the
    stuffed animal that once was mine when I, too, was interested in the
    ages of the women I love, and I say,
i'm 35, sweetie.
my oldest daughter unwraps my words and tucks them beneath her pillow,
    where fairies sometimes visit.
she crosses the days off her calendar because she is still young enough to
    believe that days can be contained by grids and tucked beneath black
    marker X's.

THE WILTED ONES

i am mother years old, infinite and enduring,
blood in your veins and thoughts in your head and bigger than myself because
        of you years old.
and I find that perhaps i too am learning to love math
  or at least the perpetual and ceaseless possibilities existing in the numbers
                      defining us.

-measuring infinity

THE WILTED ONES

dig into   the   spaces   of my ribs

the ones   as wide as   the white

between typed lines.

let me teach you how

to break   yourself   open

to know you're still alive.

-writing

THE WILTED ONES

THE WILTED ONES

the sun kisses my face
and still
shadows spring
from my shoulder blades

the issue isn't that
i can't see light
because i can

it's just that
my body can't help
but block it.

-depression is not just the absence of happiness

THE WILTED ONES

THE WILTED ONES

frost clings to tree branches
and I think of you
bared soul reaching
and how you're forever frozen that way
        reaching
                but not quite reached.
i saw you becoming gone.
i opened my mouth
        laid poems at your feet
            paved days into your skin.
i tied back the curtains of childhood
        forced the sun between your darkness
        but perhaps
                i blinded you.
i gave you too much to hold.
your limbs were not accustomed to
the weight of possibility
        and I carved rivers against you.
after all
a parched flower only dies
if you flood it with more water
        than its roots ever learned to hold.

        -it's the wilted ones who linger

THE WILTED ONES

THE WILTED ONES

can you teach a comma to uncurl
to stop being what's glanced over
to become something that's noticed
instead of something taken for granted

can I teach her to break
free
apart
to become something more than
what they speak into silence

because I'm beginning to believe
if I straighten her spine
they'll have nothing left to say.

-spliced

THE WILTED ONES

THE WILTED ONES

In the aisle of Rite-Aid, a pack of cotton balls
catches at the edges of an old worry
while the fluorescent store lights give way
to the flick of a Bic lighter
burning tin foil into scraps that litter
your closet floor like candy wrappers
where your bent frame resembles
nothing more than a pile of laundry:
a worn and crumpled thing
dirtied and discarded

and if years later
this still haunts my mind
is it any wonder
there's so little left of yours

-on the other side of addiction

THE WILTED ONES

THE WILTED ONES

dear child
you may close your eyes
stitch up your mouth
turn your back

and I will still see you
because hearts
are never quiet.

-mirror mirror

THE WILTED ONES

THE WILTED ONES

you made an autumn home of me
settled   d   e   e   p   into my center
so i tucked in tight
and i
       f
           e
              l
                 l   into being a
                   sacrifice for you

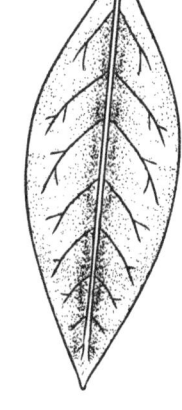

and i curled around the edges of
what i found beautiful
even though i knew

it was
      d
       y
     i
      n   g

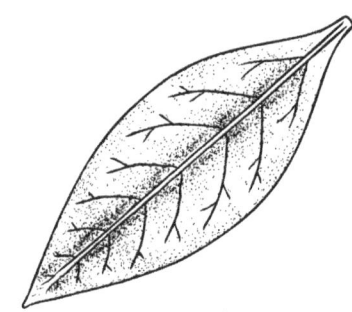

-you're still my favorite season

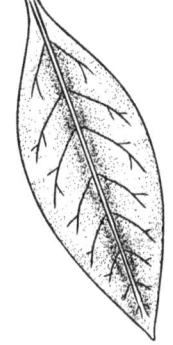

THE WILTED ONES

THE WILTED ONES

women are not a garden.
we are not just pretty things hoping to be plucked.
we do not need to be cultivated and coaxed into
opening for you.
we are the earth itself.
we are the grit roots hold to.
we are the very thing that
created you in the first place.

-i am more than you know

THE WILTED ONES

it's not the gun;
    it's the person behind it.
just like it's not the fists,
    it's the alcohol.
it's not the rape,
    it's the skirts.
it's not his skin,
    it's the hood.
just like it's not biology,
    it's a choice.
it's not news,
    it's fake.
because it's not the problem.
    you are.

-american systemic

THE WILTED ONES

2000

    he pushed me against a bed
    scraped the skin of my spine
    held my wrists and said,
        this is what couples do

2002

    he sat, tie grazing the cafeteria table
    mustache melting around his question
        so, boys,
        do you think she's still a virgin
    and when my friends refused to answer
    my teacher smiled and told them
    I must not be
    given the way I walk

2005

    stumbling home in heels too high
    and feet heavy with cranberry stains
    a strange hand groping as if
    two people passing on the sidewalk
    normally touch private things for
    the public to see
    i woke with a bruise

2006

    proctoring the first standardized test
    of my teaching career
    the male student in row two
    beckoned me to him, pointer finger
    casually calling me to walk closer

THE WILTED ONES

  to lean in until he whispered,
    i got you to come with one finger
    imagine what i could do with two

2017

  writing a poem about a life spent
  learning silence
  i look at the list of men and boys
  who built me out of permission
  i never gave
  and know people will still say
    what do you expect
    when you're a pretty girl

     -*boys will be boys*

Published in the Recenter Press Poetry Journal: *Issue One (Spring 2019)*

THE WILTED ONES

Mother Earth molded me from red clay
then gave me a heart of rainstorms
so that every month I'd bleed rivers
to give back to her again.

Mother Earth made me a mountain
gathered the salt of my sweat and
transformed the muddiness brimming within me
to vast oceans that sang her praises.

Daughters Earth laugh with tidal waves
and love like undertow and call me *mama*
and I gather red clay in my hands
until their tributaries will come unleashed.

And Mother Earth made me mother
but she reminds me with every moon cycle
of the time I sat against continental drift
and fault lines opened inside me.

Mother Earth once promised before she gave,
and I broke like a volcano until I became a valley.
Daughters Earth remind me of the life ending
in a sanguine maelstrom before it began.

Mother Earth molded me from red clay,
taught me to tear chunks of myself to give
and put rainstorms in my heart because
mothers always love what they must always lose.

-what once was lost

THE WILTED ONES

THE WILTED ONES

what do wild horses
know of freedom
when they've never suffered
the reins

there is more to my
untethering
because you tried so long
to break me

-unbridling me

THE WILTED ONES

THE WILTED ONES

look at the
c r e v i c e s
        in me
the
 s o f t n e s s
        of my hope
the
g i v i n g
        of my skin

-this is how i bloom

THE WILTED ONES

THE WILTED ONES

she cracked spines against her palms
until the words bled from her wrists

you see, she cut herself open
because her story got too big

stanzas stuck in her throat
caesuras tangled in her stomach

because when poems are your sustenance
you eat up every line

and she wondered how she could fill herself
only to still be starving

-if your depression needs a chapbook

THE WILTED ONES

THE WILTED ONES

maybe
if i can
make a
poem in
the shape
of a bottle
like the kind
you've painted
your kidneys with
you'll wrap two fingers
around its neck, place its
edges against your lips, sip
at these syllables to acquire
their taste before tilting back
whole words at a time, until
you're swallowing lines and
not even bothering to wince
at the burn because isn't the
point to drink so much bitter
the world gets blurry and you
are nothing more than a boy
bent on becoming everything
he's always hated? so tell me
if it's worth it, the leaking of
your dreams into the dregs at
the bottom of this stereotype.

-the art of being an alcoholic

THE WILTED ONES

THE WILTED ONES

i will muddy my knees
with the work of
growing you

how could i hold you
in my palms and
keep potential

from blossoming by
not cultivating
everything

inside

-the horticulture of the classroom

THE WILTED ONES

where are you
going to go
with all of that love
you will not give
yourself

-your heart is your home

THE WILTED ONES

THE WILTED ONES

dear daughters,

someday there will be a boy
and he will be beautiful
and he will break your heart.
love him anyway.
he will teach you how
to open the cage of your ribs
and be breathless.
he will teach you how
to shed your skin when
it grows too tight.
and he will teach you
how the sky can fall.
and you will learn
when it does
you are capable of
walking on stars.

-the lessons i can't teach you

THE WILTED ONES

THE WILTED ONES

sometimes there are children
who reach for me
with bare limbs rattling,
voices raw and roaring,
their need a storm bent on
covering the world.

then there are those
whose silence strikes lightning,
who crack so slowly at the core
we don't notice until
we cannot move
without trampling on their bones.

my feet are not what rests
on your ribs;
your heart is doing that.
it's my hands that are here,
holding on, hoping
the heaviness on your tongue
does not tear you apart
before I teach you
how to grow.

-when trees guide us

THE WILTED ONES

THE WILTED ONES

my heart is a hoarder.
and i just keep stacking souls
to the ceiling of my ribs.
they are spilling out of my mouth,
leaking from my fingertips,
clogging up my ventricles.

you cannot save them all,
says the housekeeper in my brain.
she's knocking on my skull.
her broom grazes the edge of
my throat and from the center of
me i extract the one made gray
with the dust of years, the one still
clinging with gossamer threads to my lungs.
i hold her up, and dangling
from her strands are

a hundred pieces of
a hundred others

and perhaps saving her
has less to do with her life
and more to do with theirs.

-redefining my saviour complex

THE WILTED ONES

THE WILTED ONES

pretty little porcelain doll
if you cut your bangs just right maybe
you can hide what it is that made him think
you're just something to be played with

and perhaps it's the cracks in your skin
that make his look so familiar
that make you think fixing him would somehow
put you back together

for who we love is nothing more than
a reflection of what we think we deserve
and you cannot smear the lipstick on a smile
that's been patiently painted on

because he took you off the shelf
he was never supposed to
and left you there
searching for the next person
who would shatter you
and finish the job

-the damage that was done/the damage that he's doing

THE WILTED ONES

THE WILTED ONES

you sleep on my shoulder
tiny breaths of namaste
entirely giving your weight over
to the dull thumping in our chests

and I wonder
someday
whose heart will comfort you
instead of my own

and I pray the heart you choose
won't beat so hard
it breaks you
but if it does

mine will be here waiting
tiny breaths of you'll be okay
entirely taking on the weight
of the ache in our chests

a song of womanhood
rising and falling
between us

-the divine

THE WILTED ONES

THE WILTED ONES

season of growth:
spring to fall
approximately eight weeks
from seed to bloom   *adolescent blizzard years*
                                    she eats snow and stereotypes
                                    sows them in her stomach

instructions for planting:
    place in well-drained, fertile soil
    though can tolerate dry and
    poor sod conditions   *disappointment growing wild*
                                    oak doors bloom eviction notices
                                    she shuts her mouth against hope

    bury seeds one quarter inch
    deep in single rows and
    thin once first leaves show   *pencil heavy hands*
                                    smear truths across journal pages
                                    she folds them into home

harvesting the root:
    use a fork or spade to
    dig beneath the base and
    lift whole from the ground   *daddy's soaked in alcohol*
                                    brother's coaxing spoons to burn
                                  sister's dancing with delirium and she
                                                             has to

    try to uncover the
    taproot deep beneath
    the surface

                            -weeding the soul

THE WILTED ONES

THE WILTED ONES

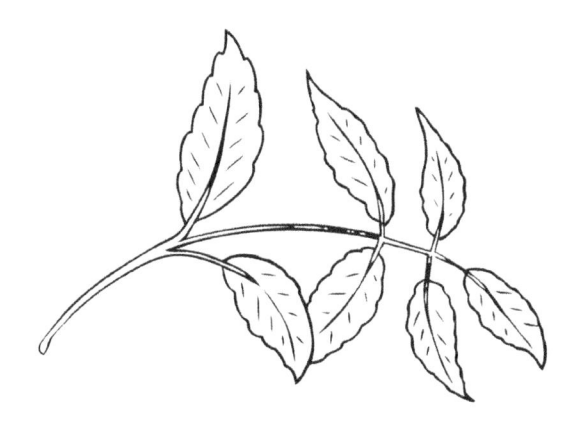

you. i write for you.
i curl like a comma
in your every breath.
i sit still as a stanza
on your skin.

i bloom vines
across your fingertips.

because you are
p   o   e   t   r   y
to me.

-inspiration is shaped like you

THE WILTED ONES

THE WILTED ONES

i bloomed out of you
and you held me straight
nourished my cut stem
kept me beautiful

until you went and broke
and the pieces of you scattered
like thorns across my days

and i know you'd tell me
i've never needed a vase
to flourish

but without you
i'm growing dry and brittle
because there's nothing here
sustaining me.

-without you i'm just broken

THE WILTED ONES

THE WILTED ONES

her hands undid me. the way they were
folded there just so,
one finger meticulously placed
above the mortcloth as if she had
plucked it over her legs herself
after crawling into the casket,
those hands that had snapped bedsheets to attention
and created hospital corners each morning she lived
because her mother had taught her a bed
isn't properly made without hospital corners
and a day isn't properly begun
until the bed is made,
and I wonder
if they've tucked the edges beneath her
the right way, first
the bottom taut and flat, then the sides
creased and straightened,
followed by excess gathered and tamed,
until the only sign that sheet
wasn't the mattress itself was the line across
each bottom corner straight as a dash
upon a tombstone,
and I can't help but think it seems
they've smoothed out her wrinkles
the way she patted out her pillows,
because I know those hands held folds
no longer visible beneath layers of makeup
meant to make her beautiful
but don't they know what made her beautiful
were the nicotine stains in her creases and
the gathering of lines across
the lengths of her fingers

THE WILTED ONES

and the liver spots pooling like sweet tea syrup
down the sides of her arms,
for what is there to say of life but that
we are no more or less
than the weathering of our skin.
so when I reached out and
placed my palm against those hands
that had shaped apple dumplings
and skimmed book pages and
planted portulacas alongside mine,
is it any wonder I thought of
hospital corners, when what I'd known had been so
scrubbed and sterilized and turned to stone
there was nothing left to do but
bury her beneath one.

-dirges (o grandmother)

Published in The Soapbox: Volume III Time
2018 PCCA Awards for Poetic Excellence Poet Laureate Winner

THE WILTED ONES

she came to me draped in buttercup petals
she plucked them from her ribs
placed them on her tongue
swallowed their poison whole
she built her immunity one truth at a time

she spoke of love like an untameable thing
wild and reaching
accustomed to breaking
untethered and overgrown

she spoke of her mother
dead
buried like a buttercup seed

she spoke of needing a mother
she stuck the silky threads of hope against my skin
and dared me to peel them free

-the moon is a reflection

THE WILTED ONES

you pour poets into my lap
who sing of the sorrow and salvation
boys bring
and i want to tell you
there is so much more to poetry
than this

-don't make your words only about them

THE WILTED ONES

THE WILTED ONES

dear daughters, part two:

I said someday there would be a boy
and I want you to know that I lied
because there may not be a boy
so much as there will be a person
and if you fall in love with a girl
when the world made you feel you shouldn't
you should love her anyway
perhaps even harder than the boy
because if there's one thing I want you to know
it's that the world has no place
breaking your heart
before love has a chance to.

-love is a person, not a gender

THE WILTED ONES

THE WILTED ONES

love is
        the ache of a girl's name on your lips
        the way you tell me you've only touched her
        when you've had too much to drink
        the pressure of your hip on mine
        the sound of your sigh at 3 am
        foreheads pressed like
        red feathers and cardinals and
        conversations with the dead
        a late night beckoning you always answer
        rain on a tin roof loud
never easy for the two of us, is it

-heart watch

THE WILTED ONES

THE WILTED ONES

there was something about the way
the words whipped about my head
as if what needed to be said
was as simple as opening my mouth
til my guts spilled out
when nothing
could be further from the truth.
I look to you and see the fire is burning low
and I know it's not as simple as
opening your mouth because
if your heart falls out
it'll shatter on this floor
and what will matter will become
nothing more than your survival
this arrival of the truth
you were never ready for
and the only way you keep breathing
is believing that stitching
the words shut and locked away
will keep the darkness hidden another day
and they won't see
they won't know
but I do--
and it's you I see
when she comes hurling back at me
a bomb of her own creation
her devastation become my own
and I run after you
your retreating view
the way I wish I could catch the wisp of her
before everything spills
like her bottle of pills

THE WILTED ONES

like your heart upon my floor
like my guts from out my mouth
and I say too much
because I'm afraid of not enough
happening on repeat and you--
you burn like her
there's something about you
I've watched die before

-as simple as

Shhhhh, the winter says to my soul.
Why not rest what's become so weary
and i tilt my head until
Okay
leaks from my thoughts.
it lays me down and
covers me tight with a blanket of snow.
it runs frigid fingers through my hair
and down the nape of my neck.
it kisses my cheeks the way
only a Mother can.
i count the lacy patterns of its crystals
icing over my eyelids,
watch the foreign fog of my breathing
erase itself in the dark,
and i almost forget how to wake
or why i should want to
when everything cold
is what feels like home.

-hibernation

THE WILTED ONES

THE WILTED ONES

i leave poems of you everywhere
    scattered like the ashes
    you so want to become.

please. i cannot knit your bones
    if they are made of dust.

-stay

THE WILTED ONES

THE WILTED ONES

this is
how i know
i am a universe.
this is how infinity
echoes in the folds of
my skin and crawls along
the stretch marks of my thighs.
this is how you are a galaxy that
will always belong to me, even after
you no longer do. because you were once
an energy, a swirl of possibility, and my body's
gravitational pull formed your kindness and etched
out your bravery (oh my dear did you know that bravery
and love are the same thing?) and burst against the under-
side of my ribs to solidify the magic of you into science.
cells like planet rings gathering until suddenly your eyes
existed and your fingers unfurled and my blood became
yours. stardust. it's still sprinkled across my abdomen,
tucked inside the moon craters surrounding my
belly button, that place where my body
unpeeled its corners, opened like a
supernova, and never quite did
smooth itself back out.
so you. here. you.
this is how
i know
god.

-the space inside of me

THE WILTED ONES

THE WILTED ONES

i press my cheek against my bathroom tiles.
coldness seeps through the spots where my arms rest.
the bruise on my left elbow, yellowed now,
reminds me of you. does your arm look like mine?
it was the first thing i thought of when that
sharp pain vibrated the crook of my elbow
and the blood bank phlebotomist
had to admit she'd nicked a nerve.
i'd wondered if that's what you felt.
i wondered how much better you were at
hitting the vein than this certified medic.
i wondered if the bruise blackening
the tributary beneath my skin
mimicked the pattern appearing on your own.
i wonder now how i could have
ignored an omen
when i bloomed one.
So i lay here, cheek to tile, bruise gone cold,
because it's all i have left of
understanding you.

-who is the real heroin(e) of your story

THE WILTED ONES

can you carve rivers
in your bones
because oceans
swallowed mine

-extinct

THE WILTED ONES

THE WILTED ONES

Trees lose everything every time the cold sets in. They stand stripped of all protection. Naked in raw winds. Soaked by snow. Ice cracking the bark barely hanging on. But the trees, they speak. The trees, they reach with their branches despite the fact they sometimes break. Your hands, the skeletons between us, this season of cold a forest of too much. But the trees. The heartbeat of hope. The way life lingers low. They grow again. Even after everything is gone, they grow again. You, the hope hanging between us, the storms rattling you. You will grow again. The trees told me so.

-seasons

THE WILTED ONES

THE WILTED ONES

her daddy scattered his brain across asphalt
caught it in motorcycle spokes
broke it against her childhood
she spent years cupping her hands around
what was left of him

her mama crawled beneath her comforter
pulled depression against her chest
poured it down her throat
she spent years soaking her palms with
what was gone in her

she sat at my feet
curled her fists to her mouth
bit at the truth imbedded there
I took her hands and said,
child, let me hold you

I scrubbed at the stains
I unclenched her fingers
I drew fireflies in their creases and said,
child, you are home

-lightning bug

THE WILTED ONES

THE WILTED ONES

let me lay literature in your lungs.
place poems behind your teeth.
let me lace your lungs with language
crack your collarbone and
unhinge your jaw.
let me give the only thing i have

these words

so you can find your own.

-come home to yourself

THE WILTED ONES

THE WILTED ONES

i'm sitting here saying goodbye
through poems you'll never see.
But i suppose i've been doing that
since the moment we met.
i suppose i've always known
losing you was a matter of *when*
instead of *if*.
and i suppose that's exactly why
i loved you in the first place.
because perhaps saving you
had less to do with your life
and more to do with
the love that should be in it.

-acceptance

THE WILTED ONES

Step One: Question
>	his hand perfectly fits mine
>	palms matched, skin pressed
>	hearts syncopated through
>	the thin layer of our connection
>	and when we move the questions
>	stuck to my tongue know the answer
>	has always been shaped
>	like him

Step Two: Research
>	friendship means
>	the poetry in his hips
>	wrapped like stanzas
>	around my thoughts
>	friendship means
>	we touch foreheads
>	instead of lips
>	friendship means
>	falling in love
>	and catching myself

Step Three: Hypothesis
>	i'll only ever believe in
>	everything he won't give

Step Four: Experiment
>	his name speaks of
>	sun and sweat, of the season
>	when everything born grows
>	and years will unravel
>	and the constellations will call out
>	an apocalypse within us
>	but i'll still lay here tracing
>	the stars on his back

THE WILTED ONES

  as if they'll guide me home
  as if stars aren't faraway bodies
  gone long before
  we pinned our wishes there

Step Five: Observations

  he holds onto me
  only where
  no one else will see
  and then
  he leaves

Step Six: Results

  he clutches girlfriends to his side
  and i wonder
  if he kisses them
  i wonder
  if their hands feel right when
  they're not mine
  i wonder
  if they can read the questions
  i buried in him
  i wonder if they answer
  what i never could

Step Seven: Communicate

  a lifetime hangs between us
  i pluck at the phrases he's choosing
  scatter them at our feet
  slip them between my lips
  how can he think this is the way
  to undo us
  when words were never
  our language

-experimental

THE WILTED ONES

the snow sticks
to the boughs of spring.
dear mother,
thank you
for reminding me
that rebirth requires
stillness.

-be patient with yourself

THE WILTED ONES

THE WILTED ONES

You
look
at
me
as if I
am air
as if I am made to

expand your lungs	nourish your bones
as if the measure of	as if the sum total of
my worth stems from	my existence curls into
how fully I can dissipate	how empty your space is
does it matter that craving me	does it matter if saving you
is a kind of self-consumption	is a kind of self-destruction
because every time you bring	because every time I unleash
me to your lips you pull me in	you in my veins I push me out
inhale me, unfiltered, until all	exhale us, nicotined, against all
that is left is the subtle scent of	that is left beneath screams of
what we were before you used	what we could have been before
up all the oxygen in the room	downing your decay like candy
before you transformed me	before you rearranged me
into nothing more than	into everything except
something so easy	something too hard
to discard.	to keep.

-aspirate

THE WILTED ONES

continents shift between our tongues.
you are intent on exploring the way
my limbs bend and my valleys arc.
you survey the curve of these borderlines
like a conqueror
        but not a settler.

you see, you fail to notice
the grit beneath my teeth,
the shifting in my skin,
the glaciers in my veins.
worlds lost because
you'll never settle.

and you, you survey me as if I
harbor gold instead of love.
possibilities drift and drown in your wake,
leave me exposed yet unknown,
a territory claimed
        but forever unsettled.

for you can possess empires
without ever creating a home.

-territory

Published in The Soapbox Volume II: Home

THE WILTED ONES

THE WILTED ONES

i lose things.
the caps of pens.
my train of thought.

you.

-the last place i looked

THE WILTED ONES

THE WILTED ONES

her fingers type, pause, type
backspace
try again
letters form, disappear, reemerge
    there are questions in every space
she's done the dance with doubt so often
others think she's waltzing
others think she never missteps

how effortless it must be for her to find the words
when they lay so thick in her throat
there's thousands to pluck free
right

her fingers grasp, release, reach
clutch at air
try again
she unravels, tidies up, tucks away

how effortless it is for her to lose herself
when no one has been trying to find her
there's thousands of things to be
right

except   of course   herself

her fingers have held
others' instructions for so long
she almost forgot she is
a poem

-draft five

THE WILTED ONES

THE WILTED ONES

In sixth grade I sat beside a boy named Donny.
Donny reminded me of Alston, a boy whose
second grade heart I'd broken
and who then moved to Idaho
before I could string an apology around it,
and so I'd bestowed the kindness I owed to Alston
on Donny, regret transferred from one
small blond head to another.
In the fall of sixth grade, Donny died.
A car clipped him while he was getting mail
from the mailbox on his street.
My regret scattered like the leaves framing his still face.
I scooped up the pieces and gathered them like
a makeshift memorial around his empty desk.
I wound words around his absence, and I learned why
people speak in cliches, because I wrote them,
my middle school pencil
tracing the tragedy weighing down our tongues,
calling the boy I barely knew "our hero,"
as if he had sacrificed himself
at the altar of our budding adolescence.
As if he'd stepped in front of that car
to save us from the perils of our innocence.
In seventh grade, Steven died.
His bike flew from that alley as if it could burn its way
into a phoenix, as if the car that hit his frail body
would explode it into ashes so Steven would arise again,
perhaps into a life where someone paid attention.
But instead that accident squashed him into two dimensions,
a black and white yearbook photo I only remember
because we used it again our senior year, a little boy
on the precipice of our adulthood.

THE WILTED ONES

Middle school became an experiment in reality.
I stared at the grains of the playground asphalt
and wondered how we weren't all six feet beneath it.
Years later, after stumbling upon my fifth grade yearbook,
I'd open the front cover to discover Steven's signature
tucked directly below Donny's.
No one else's signature spilled into theirs, as if the
kinetic energy of the ink they'd used pushed everyone away
from the fates inscribed there.
I traced the outlines of their names, placed the book on its spine
as if to make it a monument, this little wall dedicated to
the war of our childhood and its victims,
this being all that I really have left.
In my second year of teaching, Jimmy died.
In my third, Lizzy plucked pills and placed them between her lips like candy.
In my tenth, Kory crumpled to his bathroom floor,
the cap and gown he'd worn a few years earlier now limp
upon a hanger, gathering dust in a corner.
A note from him sits in my bottom desk drawer.
School for me has always been a balancing act of
beginnings brimming over and empty desks dripping.
I am turning over faces like pages, finding roadmaps in
their irises, warning signs I can lay before the ones still here
like tarot cards or blueprints or sixth grade window-panes
because what more can I teach but that we lose what we love
and we must still love, anyway. We must keep living, anyway.
I teach literature because it sings of the strings that bind,
of the short spaces between potential and impermanence,
of the way answers are never clear or the same for any of us.
I teach poetry and stories and novels
because what we read is timeless in a way we never can be.
Because what we create is all that is ever left.

-the strings that bind

THE WILTED ONES

with cups lining the shelves,
secondhand, prices untagged,
open your hands to trace their rims;
take one up, turn it over,
consider the tea stains
settled in the fine ceramic cracks,
the paisley pattern worn bare in its center,
the chips littering the lip of its base.
ask me the cost of finding what
no one else looks for.
measure its weight, the heft of its build,
curl fingertips around the handle;
linger there a bit
amidst the remnants of other palms
from other places, holding this mug,
tea bags steeping, tongues burnt in
impatience or curiosity or need,
before placing the vessel
back in its place
and walking away empty-handed.

-thrift shop heart

THE WILTED ONES

THE WILTED ONES

she stared at the way the light muted itself
against the tan bottle, bent her hand
to hold it in her palms
counted the number of pills inside
broke her depression against their edges
one, two, twenty later
and the light blared against her retinas
and perhaps pain is easier when there's a reason for it
she opened her mouth and spit out confessions

she felt so invisible
she felt so exposed
she wanted to just cup the light until she could see it
but all she found was a void
the empty chair sits silent as she was
why is it we only see her after she's not here

THE WILTED ONES

and now she exists between muted walls
white coats and soft tones where she dissects her insides
they ask questions like equations
as if the answers were so readily charted
they spill her into another manila folder
and hand her a tan bottle with her name on it
tell her to count the pills inside
repair what you damaged
they drip diagnoses across her skin until
one, two, a thousand capsules later
she feels so invisible
she feels so exposed
that she wonders if light really exists at all
or if it's just another figment of chemical imbalance
because how can it be
the way she tried to end it
is the only way they tell her
she'll be able to survive it

why is it we only see her after she's gone

-prescribed

i held his name under my tongue
like a prayer, like a confession,
like his chest was an altar i'd worshipped
but could never bring myself to touch
i studied the psalms of his lips
and held him in the palms of my hands
like rosary beads, like a hymn,
like a forbidden fruit i placed against my teeth
but never brought myself to bite
and i cannot tell if he's god
or the snake

-religion moves like you

THE WILTED ONES

THE WILTED ONES

forgive me when
i am less mother
and more human

i know not
the damage i do

i'll forget that
unraveling my heart
only winds it around
your feet

or i'll realize this
and continue

to spout verses and
write you a bible bent on
reminding you
not to judge
what you're destined to
one day
become

-repentance

THE WILTED ONES

love sticks
to the back of your throat
and coats everything
you try to say

-nonverbal

THE WILTED ONES

THE WILTED ONES

tell me i'm pretty.
strip me down to the barest truth.
lay me open before you with my
cracked spine and gilded cover,
my mascaraed eyes and contoured doubt.
notice the rise in my hips,
the curve of my waist,
the ink stains of my irises.
close my eyes, please, to
how i should want to be
so much more than this.
make my skin your favorite meal.
trace every inch of my surface.
please.
make me forget
what's beneath it.

-remedy

THE WILTED ONES

THE WILTED ONES

he wrote to me of the rain.
i can see him there, droplets against the windshield,
wondering how it is you can love
what was never meant to be yours.
he wants to reach over, grab the hand of the boy
in the passenger seat, make him see
what's right in front of him.
he wants to explain how he has been lost
and searching for words in a language
that wasn't his native tongue and that this boy
is translation. this boy is home country.
this boy is resurrection. but this boy is searching for places
the rain doesn't touch. this boy is wanderlust.
this boy is looking everywhere but at him.
his hands are on the steering wheel and he thinks perhaps
this moment can be enough,
the two of them alone in the world, between destinations.
he's stealing minutes and tucking them under his tongue,
he's pasting himself together with small glances but
it's 2 am and everything is blurry. and
silence places its finger to his lips, presses
against the space widening between them as
he pulls into the boy's driveway, and watches him walk away.
he wrote to me of the rain.
and how it's all he ever really had.
at home, the pills drop like water against a windshield.
look how they fill the empty spaces of his hands.
he tucks them beneath the desk, buries them where
only he can see, and stumbles back to his silence
once again.

-love is blind

THE WILTED ONES

THE WILTED ONES

losing you made me
a home for heartbreak.
you took the hinges
when you took your life,
and so now the door
flings wide open,
welcoming any tragedy
needing a place to stay.

-the legacy of your suicide

THE WILTED ONES

softness
is the bravest skin
you can wear

-always, feel

THE WILTED ONES

THE WILTED ONES

he's young and thinks love
must be tragic to be real.

he texts the boy he wants as more
than just another boy who can't admit
he wants another boy.

he takes him to cliffs overlooking
the countryside mountains
of their little hometown
and imagines how it would be to kiss him.

the boy tells him to ask what it is
he wants to know but
he's young and thinks love
must be tragic to be real
so he doesn't ask everything
tripping over itself in his throat
and he coughs up confessions
that almost admit how badly he wants this boy
to be so much more than just another boy.

almost. because you cannot answer
the questions never asked. and there's
so much more of home in this uncertainty
than there would be in the knowing and so
he imagines kissing this boy
and stays still as a statue, a monument in
his own museum of close encounters.
he sits near him and sleeps beside him
and has felt his skin against his own

THE WILTED ONES

and yet
and yet.

his boy is another boy who can't admit
he wants another boy
and isn't that tragic;
isn't that so real
it hurts.

and he's young, and he believes
this is what it means
to love. and so he never asks, anyway.

-what is and what shall never be

THE WILTED ONES

                    l o
                v   e
                            stings
                                like
                            menthol
                    cigarettes
                            trailing the
                                length
                        of her
                            childhood in
                                    wispy
                            strands of
                    her
                        g
                         r
                          a
                              n
                                d
                                m
                                 o
                                  t
                                 h
                                  e r

and she is staring at the space where the weeping willow used to stand, solid as the woman who had planted it. chainsaw screeches, dropping limbs, leaves, all the pieces of all she had left. the tree's lungs gasp in the autumn air, tendrils of black and blue nights escaping, dissipating, on its way to turning to ash.

-habits

THE WILTED ONES

THE WILTED ONES

a thousand women tangle in every curl of your hair.
fingertips of fermented years resting on your tongue.
open your mouth and speak.

aftertaste of ashes between your teeth.
a thousand women picking syllables from your gums.
consonants crashing into a vertebrae of verbs.
open your mouth and speak.

centuries stacked like handwritten notes.
ink trailing from your lips.
a thousand women line your cheeks.
they're pushing against your throat.
plucking at vocal chords.
daring you like sirens to
open your mouth.

and speak.

-centrifugal motion

THE WILTED ONES

THE WILTED ONES

who were you
before you had
all of me

who am i
now that i'm
all out of you

-identity theft

THE WILTED ONES

THE WILTED ONES

Emerging from the bathroom, towel wrapped tight against my chest,
I find my oldest standing there, unsure eyes and too-small nightgown.

I can't get to sleep, she mumbles, and I rub my irritation against the underside of her
anxiety, offer her crumbs of Just let me get my pajamas on before turning away.

I sigh against the frame of my own bed, throw the towel across it and pull
threadbare patience along my skin. My phone buzzes a deathsong.

I left its charger in my car, so I sneak past the cracked door of my
daughter's room, slide into the night. The sky greets me.

The vastness calls, and I am back inside, finding blankets to spread over
grass barely breathing again; I'm beckoning my oldest to grab her comforter and come here.

Come here, where the night cradles our smallness and contains light older than
anyone on earth, light still visible even though its source extinguished long ago.

Come here, under these reminders of the way love lingers long after its home is swallowed
and where your head and mine rest on the same pillow, tucked safely in the same space.

Come here, apart from what weighs heavy against my days, where I can see you better,
and listen to you truer, and believe in magic again.

THE WILTED ONES

Thank you for making me a person, my daughter whispers to the universe.

I pull her closer, hug her longer, watch the constellations catching in our
    collarbones.

Back inside, outside air clinging to the threads of our thoughts, I forget my
    exhaustion
on the floor of her childhood, and sing until her eyes close, and I linger there
    alone.

-stargazer

THE WILTED ONES

the blood pools against the underside of
her adoption, stains the spaces around
her six siblings, turns her a different
color from everyone she calls hers.
It collects metallic along her tongue
every time her name drags itself from her
mother. father. strangers. life bookmarked by
the biology of desperation.
she's bruised choices deep and only knows how
to bleed all over the linoleum.
she's pressing fingers against the damage,
spreading herself thin as broken vessels,
pouring herself into whatever shape
someone will notice. clots of attention
from everywhere but where it matters most.
paper hospital gowns scraping at knees.
nurses questioning the wounds her parents
should be. is it any wonder she seeps
into any open crevice near her?
weaving other's words into a roadmap;
custom-made DNA of what ifs and
why nots, a genetic malfunctioning
between being born and belonging, can
you see the black and blue coloration
lining her hope? ancient hurts no one can heal
as she cuts herself open with razors
and poetry and girls and a god who
taught her to equate emptiness with love.

-hematoma

THE WILTED ONES

THE WILTED ONES

you put on my lipstick and I think of the stains
on the ends of her cigarettes. ashes lining
my teeth. does she stroke your cheek, dear child? does she know?

you insist on removing your shoes, peeling your
socks free, careening barefoot across this backyard
and I wonder if you inherited her lack
of control and knack for adventure; what if you
have, and she'll slip pills beneath your tongue the same way
my poor eyesight condemned you before you were born.

do you dress in her death? when they wrap bracelets
of comparison around your wrists, do you smell
sympathy flowers on their breath? and does she know?

we speak of your future and it cracks the varnished
corners of conversations I imagine she
once had with her own mother, before she grew
out of hope and into imbalance, before she
stopped believing in the feel of curled grass against
naked toes and hope, before she became my fear.

you remind me she once was young as you and your
ability to reach an age she never did
comes with no guarantee. I worry what she knows.

-elegy for a worry

THE WILTED ONES

THE WILTED ONES

First, take stock of format.
Check the use of white space, the
v   o   i   d
between each rib.
discover what is being said

                                    the body carries trauma

by what is left unsaid.

Focus then on punctuation.
Where are you asked to pause,
       consider,
              fully halt,

                                pressure points like commas

and where do words simply move
      connect

THE WILTED ONES

        wholly unleash

                      handprints bone deep

Are you told what is meant
    or must you leave room
        for interpretation

                      skin unraveling in ink

And then, perhaps, after this,
you are ready to roll the language
about your tongue.

                      living between commas

Savor what is offered to you, what
d   r   i   p   s
down the page
    across fingers
        through veins
taste what remains

                      the body carries trauma

long after
    the end.

       -how to analyze a poem (or, how to diagnose the damage)

*2019 PCCA Awards for Poetic Excellence Poet Laureate Winner

THE WILTED ONES

a squirrel scampers across our yard and you
exclaim a thousand languages to it,
matching syllables to its tail twitches.

you steal brown markers from your sister's room
and declare them green or maybe yellow
because everything means what you decide it does.

you crawl into my lap and press your cheek to mine
because love is a cloth we weave
and I feel like home. you are home.

-inhabitant

THE WILTED ONES

THE WILTED ONES

when he bruised her arm
did he notice
the color of the church pews

when he split open her holy
did he realize
the ghost he unleashed inside

when he emptied her
did she bleed
like a sacrificial lamb

she's been a walking apology
for his damage

with no god left
to answer

-tithing

THE WILTED ONES

THE WILTED ONES

TV taught me to see color
  by taking it away,
making the world suddenly
      black
         and white.
I sat on the floor,
crayons scattered around,
      reds and yellows,
         vibrant blues;
rainbows ran before my eyes
  like pixels on paper
as the news announced
words I didn't understand:
      Courtroom Evidence
and
      Racial Divide.
I looked up to see a picture,
    a photograph,
    a couple,
and I clutched my crayons
as the people talking
called them
    black
    and white
instead of
    man and woman.
And suddenly,
I saw the skin
of what they meant
while confusion colored me
at the shades of difference

THE WILTED ONES

      being drawn.
The contrast crackled
like static on the station;
the crayons cascaded
  from my careful grip.
      The colors broke,
        the news went on,
and the world was reduced
to what TV
      taught me to see.

        -colored

2016 Sophie Awards for Poetic Excellence Poet Laureate Winner

THE WILTED ONES

what is this ancient song
boiling in my blood
making me older than centuries,
vast as oceans?

I am parched ground
hungry and open
ready and reaching
for hurricane season.
why does this tempest
only spin tantrums
around my ribs

because oh how I flood
how I drown
how I live a thousand lives
drenched to my core

how I've shivered
and stared at the way
the sun licks my skin
but never stays

because don't you know
I'm thick as fog
so unsubstantial
in my sadness

can I bleed for you
rub myself raw
drop these stories like
stems no longer welcome

THE WILTED ONES

where they once grew

why is it
my favorite time of year
is this fall
into the depths of me,
this burrowing
straight through my bones,
this unraveling
that leaves me bare as
branches reaching out
instead of curling in

what is this ancient thing
making me feel
beautiful
and ugly
from different sides
of the same mouth

-the ruins

THE WILTED ONES

I look at myself
and I can only see
what I don't want to

I look at you
look at me
in that way that makes me
beautiful again

and how do you thank someone
for seeing what you can't
for giving you the lenses
for refracting the shadows
just in time
every time

-husband

THE WILTED ONES

THE WILTED ONES

my neighbor washes her hair
outside in November
as the numbers dip below her
knees and autumn tumbles
past her toes.
the wind chill chases the white
strands spilling from her neck
when she turns her head
toward her shins,
bowing in gratitude to the
brisk air for filling her lungs
once more.

my neighbor plays piano by lamplight in the middle room of her house.
i've seen her sitting there at 4:00 a.m., bent over keys
worn as her spine. i've closed my eyes and let the notes seep through
the brick and mortar and bones. i've rocked my babies back to sleep
with her muffled music swaddled about us.

my neighbor wears oven mitts as gloves
because the ice crystals of a nor'easter can burn fingertips
as easily as oven racks or Indian summer afternoons.
cracks line her cheeks more deeply than the asphalt of
this street she has walked every frigid morning of my waking.

my neighbor cements herself a signpost of my childhood.
she blooms across the years spanning between our bodies
like the magnolia shedding blossoms in her front yard.
i find petals stuck to my soles like dog-eared pages.
i watch for her huddled form in my frosted breath.

THE WILTED ONES

my neighbor thinks my name is Lauren.
but i never correct her, because she brings me apples
and paper plates of tiny Christmas cookies
and a sense that age and time and names are nothing more
than markers of man. but home is a woman

in a Pennsylvania town
with hands that have held lifetimes
in me.

-home is a person you never knew

THE WILTED ONES

because you cannot keep me
anymore than i can keep you
i'll weave words
i'll string pages together
i'll hold you in my hands like an offering

a letting go of what i can't hold
a giving of yourself to you

-finis

THE WILTED ONES

ACKNOWLEDGEMENTS

thank you
heartache
for teaching me to love
and lose
and keep loving anyway

thank you
love
for making a home for me
in all of the people
who gave me roots

there would be no poetry
without this

THE WILTED ONES

ABOUT THE AUTHOR

Lynne Reeder lives through words. She writes them, reads them, teaches them, and believes in them always. When she isn't in her high school classroom or wrangling her two daughters, Lynne manages to write; her work has appeared on *Mothers Always Write, By Me Poetry, Worldwide Poetry,* and *Make Blackout Poetry,* and she has been published in *Genre Urban Arts, The Soapbox Volume II* and *III, [Insert Yourself Here]* (The Paragon Journal), *I Have a Name* (Creative Talents Unleashed), and *Strange Magic* (Sunbury Press), and various other journals and anthologies. A collection of Lynne's writings and blackout poetry, *Found Between the Lines,* and her first chapbook, *Featherstone,* are available now. She also writes a column and blog for *Central Penn Parent Magazine.* She resides in her childhood hometown in central Pennsylvania with her husband and girls, where she holds the title of Perry County Poet Laureate. Learn more about Lynne and her works at www.lynnereeder.com.

Instagram: @thepoemreeder
Facebook: Lynne Reeder, Poet & Author
Twitter: @thepoemreeder